Buddhist Paintings coloring book

Buddhism is a set of beliefs and practices that follows the teachings of Siddhartha Gautama, a young prince who lived in northern India or Nepal around 2,500 years ago. Stories passed down through generations tell of how Siddhartha gave up his comfortable life at the royal palace and wandered the land, living among the common people and witnessing much human suffering. This experience led him on a quest to find release from the cycle of suffering. He studied with wise teachers but still did not find the answer. Finally, he decided to meditate (sit in quiet thought) until the answer came to him. After 49 days he finally achieved enlightenment, or attainment of wisdom. Then he attained Buddhahood ("Buddha" means "enlightened one" in Sanskrit, one of the languages of India and Asia) and spent the rest of his life teaching what he had discovered. Since that time, Buddhism has spread worldwide.

The twenty-two pictures in this coloring book depict many figures important in Buddhism, from compassionate deities (gods) to humble abbots (heads of monasteries) to wise *arhats* (disciples of the Buddha entrusted with propagating and protecting Buddhist beliefs). The original artworks are shown on the inside covers. When you color the pictures, you can follow the colors used in the original works or choose your own. The last page of the book is blank, for you to draw your own spiritual guide. Would it be a person from your school or place of worship? Or perhaps an imaginary being who watches out for you?

ASIAN ART MUSEUM
CHONG-MOON LEE CENTER
FOR ASIAN ART AND CULTURE

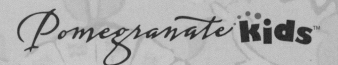

All works of art are in the collection of the Asian Art Museum of San Francisco.

1. Guardian King of the West, 2002–2003. By Seol Min (Korean, b. 1966). Hanging scroll, ink and colors on cotton, 136¼ x 85½ in. (image/overall). Gift of Jae-u, 2004.10. © Buddhist nun Seol Min. Courtesy of the Asian Art Museum.

2. The Buddhist guardian Skanda (Korean: Dongjin Bosal), 2008. By Myung Chun (Korean, b. 1962). Hanging scroll, ink and colors on hemp, 79 x 35⅝ in. (overall). Gift of Monk Myung Chun, 2008.12. © Buddhist monk Myung Chun. Courtesy of the Asian Art Museum.

3. White-robed Water-Moon Avalokiteshvara, 2008. By Seol Min (Korean, b. 1966). Hanging scroll, ink and colors on cotton, 92½ x 73 in. (image), 114 x 79 in. (overall). Gift of Seol Min, 2008.11. © Buddhist nun Seol Min. Courtesy of the Asian Art Museum.

4. The Diamond (Kongokai) Mandala, one of the Two World (Ryokai) Mandalas (detail), probably 1700–1800. Japan. Edo period (1615–1868). One of a pair of hanging scrolls, ink, colors, and gold on silk, 40¾ x 35¾ in. (image). Gift of Gary Snyder, 2004.8.

5. The monk Hva-shang and the Buddhist guardians Virudhaka and Dhritarashtra (detail), 1800–1900. Tibet. Thangka (first in a series of seven), colors on cotton, 23¾ x 17 in. The Avery Brundage Collection, B62D44.

6. The Buddhist guardian Gompo, 2003. By Pema Tenzin. Bhutan. Colors and gold on cotton, 39½ x 27 in. (image). Acquisition made possible by Tibetan Study Group, 2004.29.

7. Mandala with thunderbolts (detail), 1800–1900. Mongolia. Colors on cotton, 18⅛ x 14¼ in. (image). Gift of Frederic B. and Philippi H. Butler, B85D2.

8. The arhat Gopaka (detail). Khams region, Tibet, eighteenth century. Ink and colors on cotton, 41 x 23¾ in. The Avery Brundage Collection, B61D1+.

9. The guardian deity Weituo. China, c. sixteenth century, Ming dynasty (1368–1644). Ink and colors on silk, 66¼ x 38½ in. Transfer from the Fine Arts Museums of San Francisco. Gift of Albert M. Bender, B80D3.

10. The protective deity Yama (detail). Tibet, eighteenth century. Ink and colors on cotton, 52½ x 29 in. The Avery Brundage Collection, B60D25.

11. The arhats Panthaka, Nagasena, Gopaka, and Abheda (detail). Tibet, c. nineteenth century. Sixth in a series of seven images, ink and colors on cotton, 23¾ x 17 in. The Avery Brundage Collection, B62D41.

12. Maitreya, the Buddha of the Future, 1800–1900. Tibet. Colors and gold on cotton, 94 x 53 in. (overall). The Avery Brundage Collection, B60D54.

13. The Buddhist arhats Rahula, Chuda-panthaka, and Pindola-bharadvaja (detail), approx. 1800–1900. Tibet. Fifth in a series of seven paintings, colors on cotton, 23¾ x 17 in. (image). The Avery Brundage Collection, B62D42.

14. The Buddha Amitayus, 1779. China; Chengde, Hebei province. Qing dynasty, reign of the Qianlong emperor (1736–1795). Colors on cotton, 64 x 37 in. (overall). The Avery Brundage Collection, B60D24.

15. A vision of the great lama Tsongkha-pa as the deity Dombi-Heruka. Tibet, eighteenth century. Thangka, colors on cotton, 58 x 34 in. (overall). The Avery Brundage Collection, B62D37.

16. The Buddhist deity White Tara. Tibet, nineteenth century. Thangka, colors on cotton, 47 x 30 in. (overall). Gift of Katherine Ball, B72D44.

17. The Buddhist guardian king Vaishravana, c. 1650–1700. Tibet; Shalu monastery, Tsang region. Thangka, colors on cotton, 65 x 35 in. (overall). The Avery Brundage Collection, B60D53.

18. Death of the Buddha, twentieth century. Tibet. Thangka, colors on cotton, 39½ x 24 in. (overall). The Avery Brundage Collection, B66D23.

19. The bodhisattva Samantabhadra (detail), 1779–1780. China; Xumifushou Temple, Chengde, Hebei province. Qing dynasty, reign of the Qianlong emperor (1736–1795). Thangka, colors on cotton, 83 x 37½ in. (overall). Gift of Katherine Ball, B72D67.

20. The Buddhist abbot Buton Rinchen Drup, c. 1650–1700. Tibet; Tsang region. Hanging scroll, ink on silk, 66 x 42½ in. (overall). The Avery Brundage Collection, B60D38.

21. A vision of the abbot Tsong Khapa as the bodhisattva Manjushri, c. 1700. Tibet. Hanging scroll, ink on silk, 58½ x 33 in. (overall). The Avery Brundage Collection, B62D33.

22. Portrait of Seosan Taesa (1520–1604). Korea, 1550–1700; Joseon dynasty (1392–1910). Hanging scroll, ink and colors on silk, 75 x 37⅞ in. (overall). Museum purchase, City Arts Trust Fund, 1992.345.

Pomegranate Communications, Inc.
Box 808022, Petaluma CA 94975
800 227 1428
www.pomegranate.com

Pomegranate Europe Ltd.
Unit 1, Heathcote Business Centre, Hurlbutt Road
Warwick, Warwickshire CV34 6TD, UK
[+44] 0 1926 430111
sales@pomeurope.co.uk

© 2009 Asian Art Museum / Chong-Moon Lee Center for Asian Art and Culture

Catalog No. CB111

Designed by Stephanie Odeh

Printed in Korea

1. Guardian King of the West

2. The Buddhist guardian Skanda

3. White-robed Water-Moon Avalokiteshvara

5. The monk Hva-shang and the Buddhist guardians Virudhaka and Dhritarashtra (detail)

6. The Buddhist guardian Gompo

7. Mandala with thunderbolts (detail)

8. The arhat Gopaka (detail)

9. The guardian deity Weituo

10. The protective deity Yama (detail)

11. The arhats Panthaka, Nagasena, Gopaka, and Abheda (detail)

12. Maitreya, the Buddha of the Future

13. The Buddhist arhats Rahula, Chuda-panthaka, and Pindola-bharadvaja (detail)

14. The Buddha Amitayus

15. A vision of the great lama Tsongkha-pa as the deity Dombi-Heruka

16. The Buddhist deity White Tara

17. The Buddhist guardian king Vaishravana

18. Death of the Buddha

19. The bodhisattva Samantabhadra (detail)

20. The Buddhist abbot Buton Rinchen Drup

21. A vision of the abbot Tsong Khapa as the bodhisattva Manjushri

22. Portrait of Seosan Taesa

Draw and color your own picture here!